Finding Alaska

Artistic Images of Land Creatures…
to Color!

Brittney Kauffman

Inkedfoxbybrittney.com
www.facebook.com/artbybrittneyk
inkedfoxak@gmail.com

Guidelines

1. Gently tear or cut the page of your choosing out of the coloring book.

2. Color your page using colored pencils, fine-tip markers, or fine-tip pens. It's your art, so these are just suggestions. (I personally use Staedtler marker pens)

3. Find the word 'Alaska' hidden in your drawing.

4. Display! Each page is 8x10 and one-sided for the purpose of being able to display your work. (8x10 is also a standard frame size)

Most of all, Have fun!

Can't find 'Alaska' in your drawing? Look to the back of the book for help!

Dedicated to my family, friends, and fans who have supported me and my art.
Cover photo colored by Brian Svedin

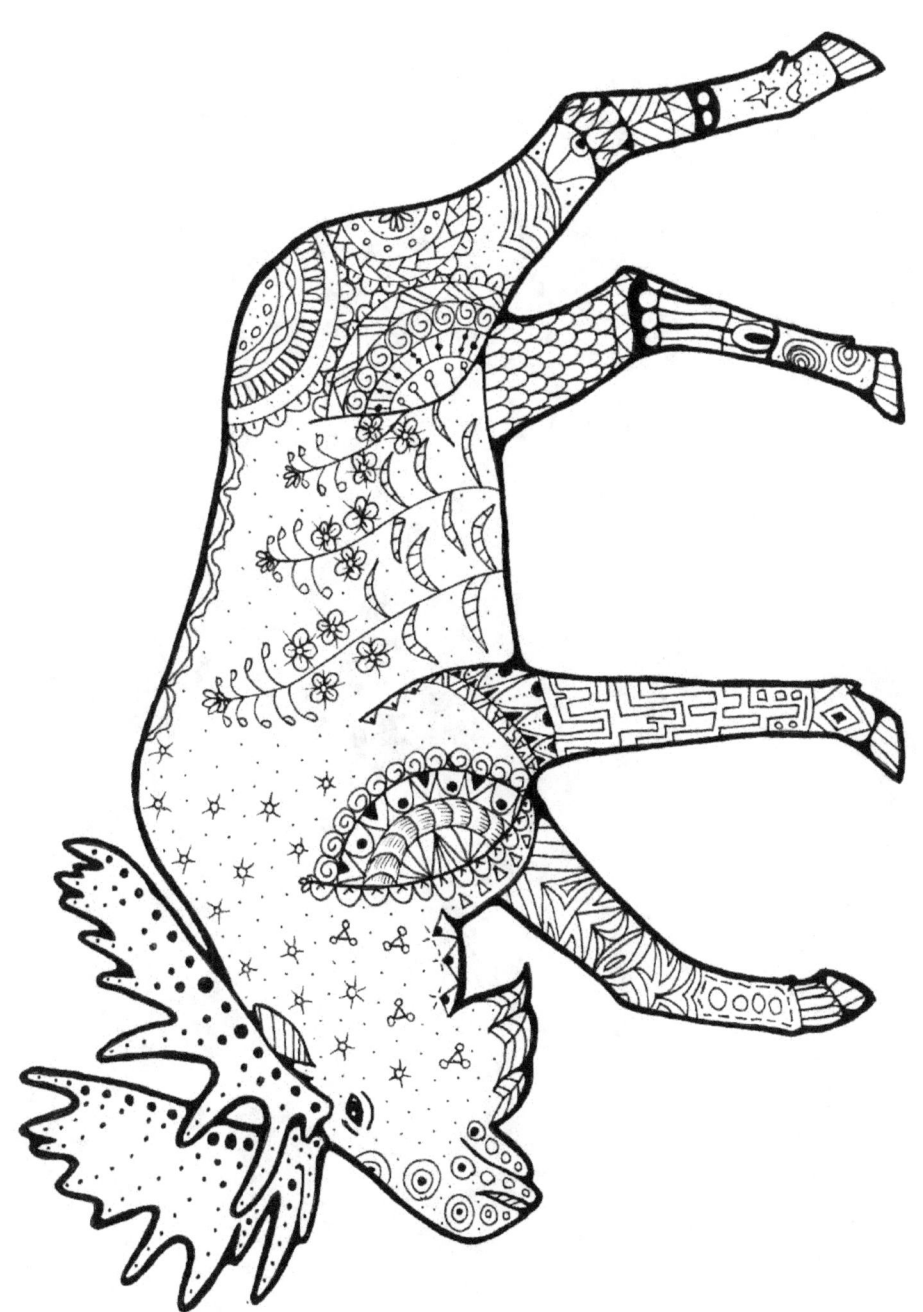

Bull Moose

Fun Fact: An adult moose can grow up to around
6.5 feet tall.

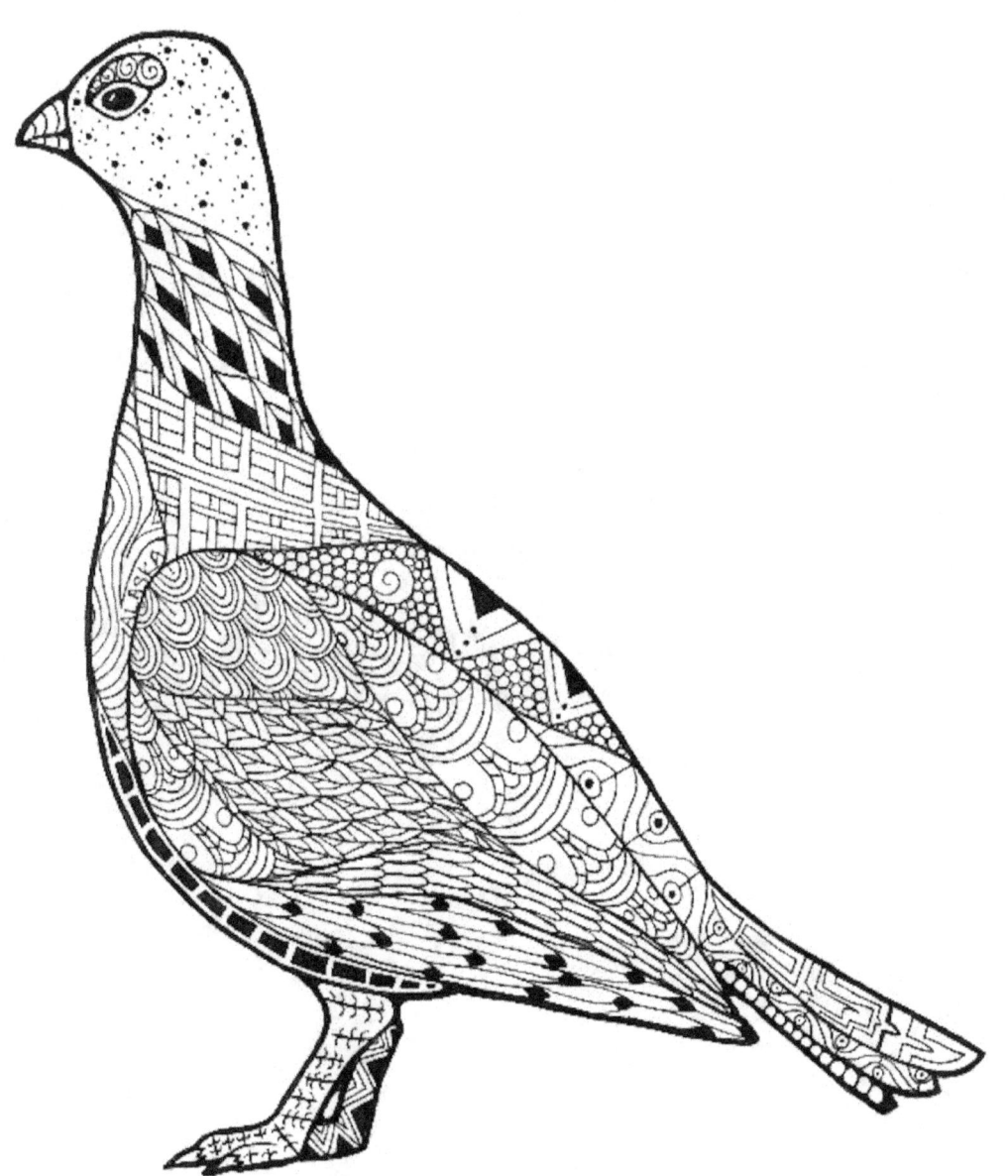

Willow Ptarmigan

Fun Fact: This is Alaska's state bird.

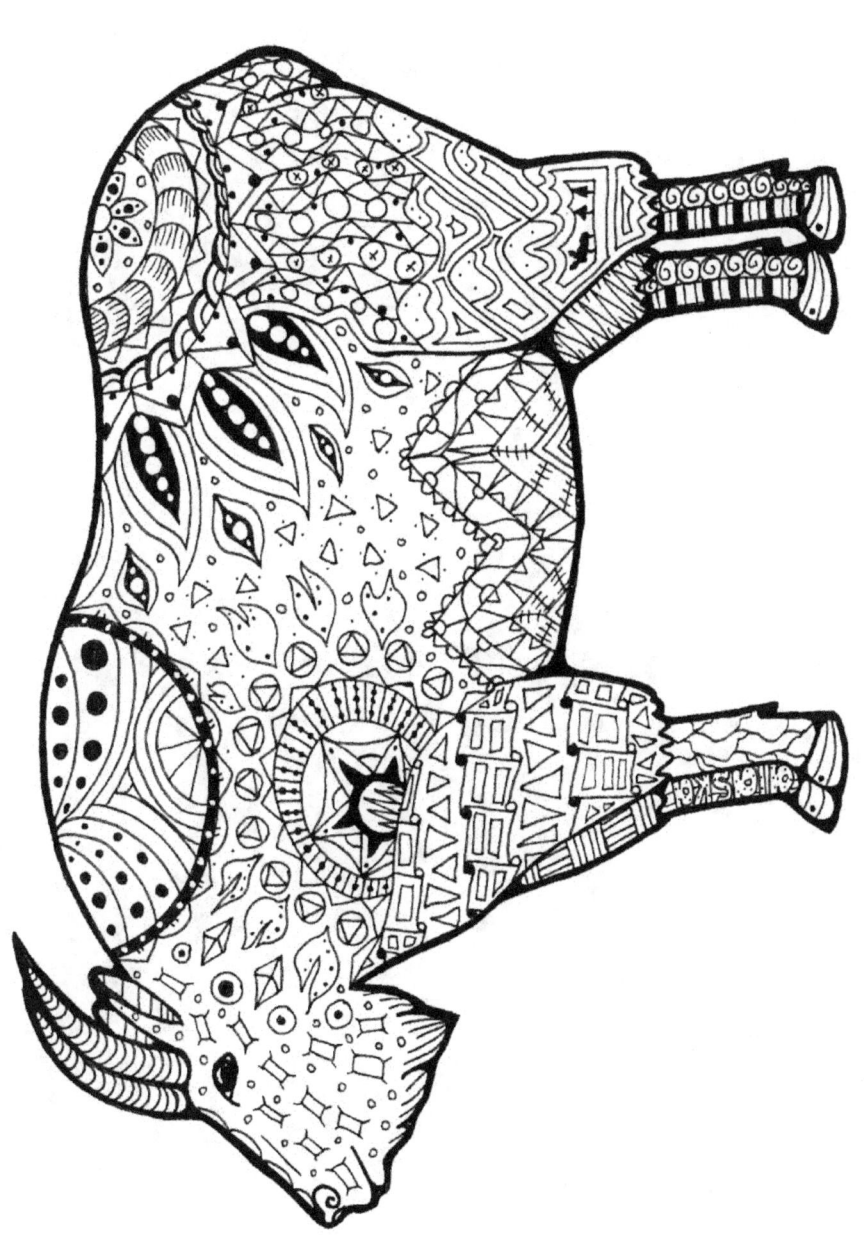

Mountain Goat

Fun Fact: Mountain goat hooves are made for navigating the rough terrain they inhabit.

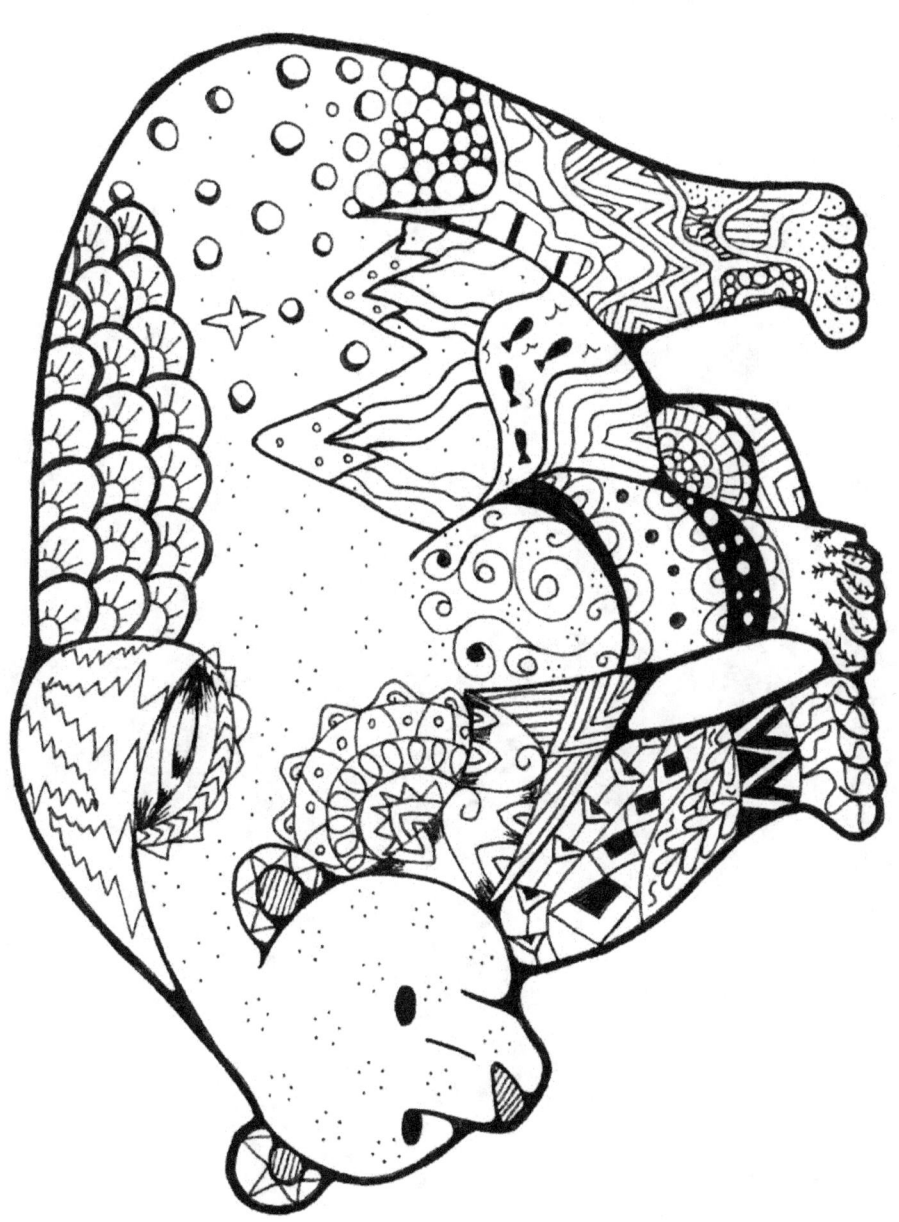

Brown Bear

Fun Fact: Brown bears are omnivores.

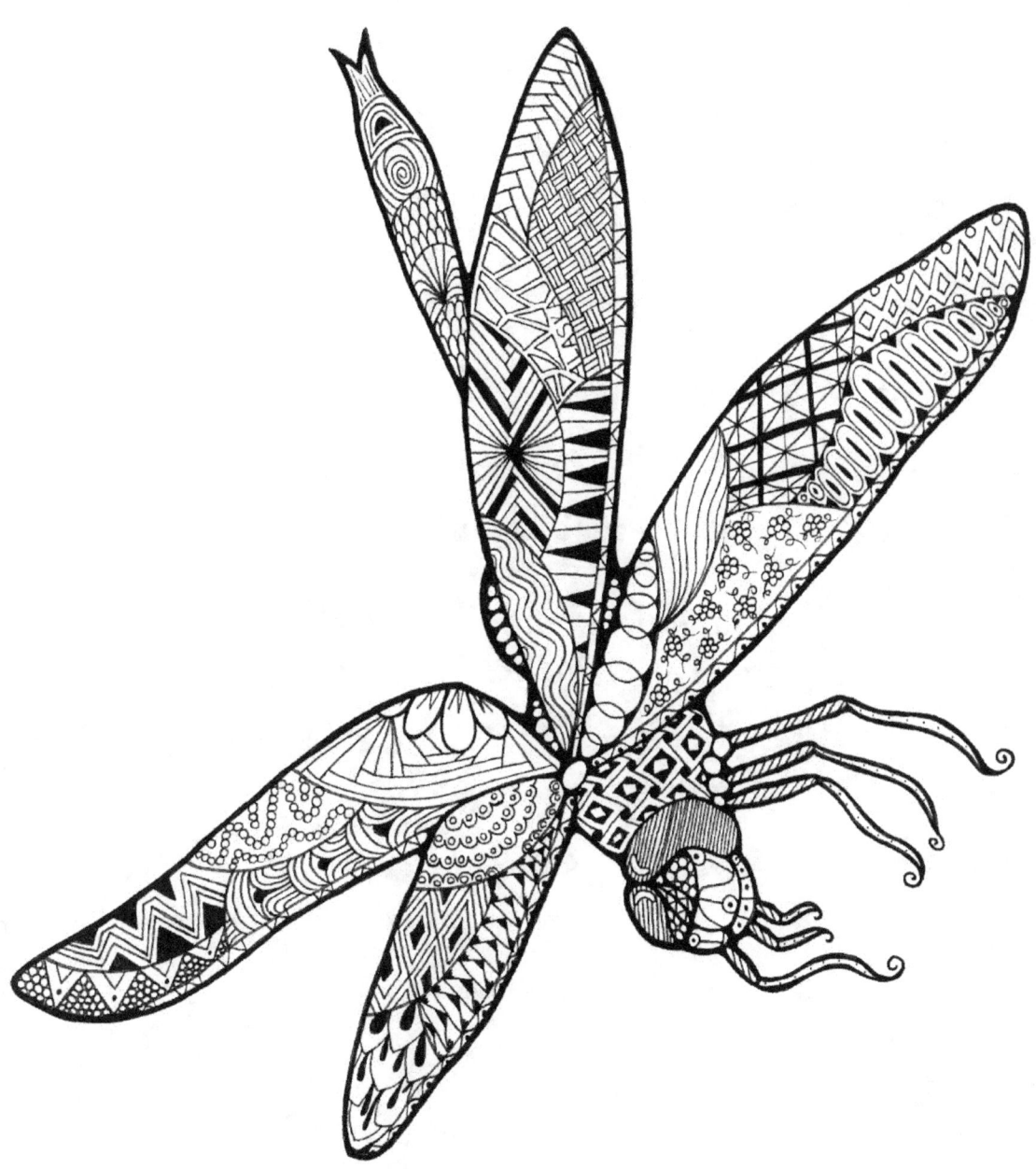

Dragonfly

Fun Fact: Adult dragonflies can grow to almost two inches long

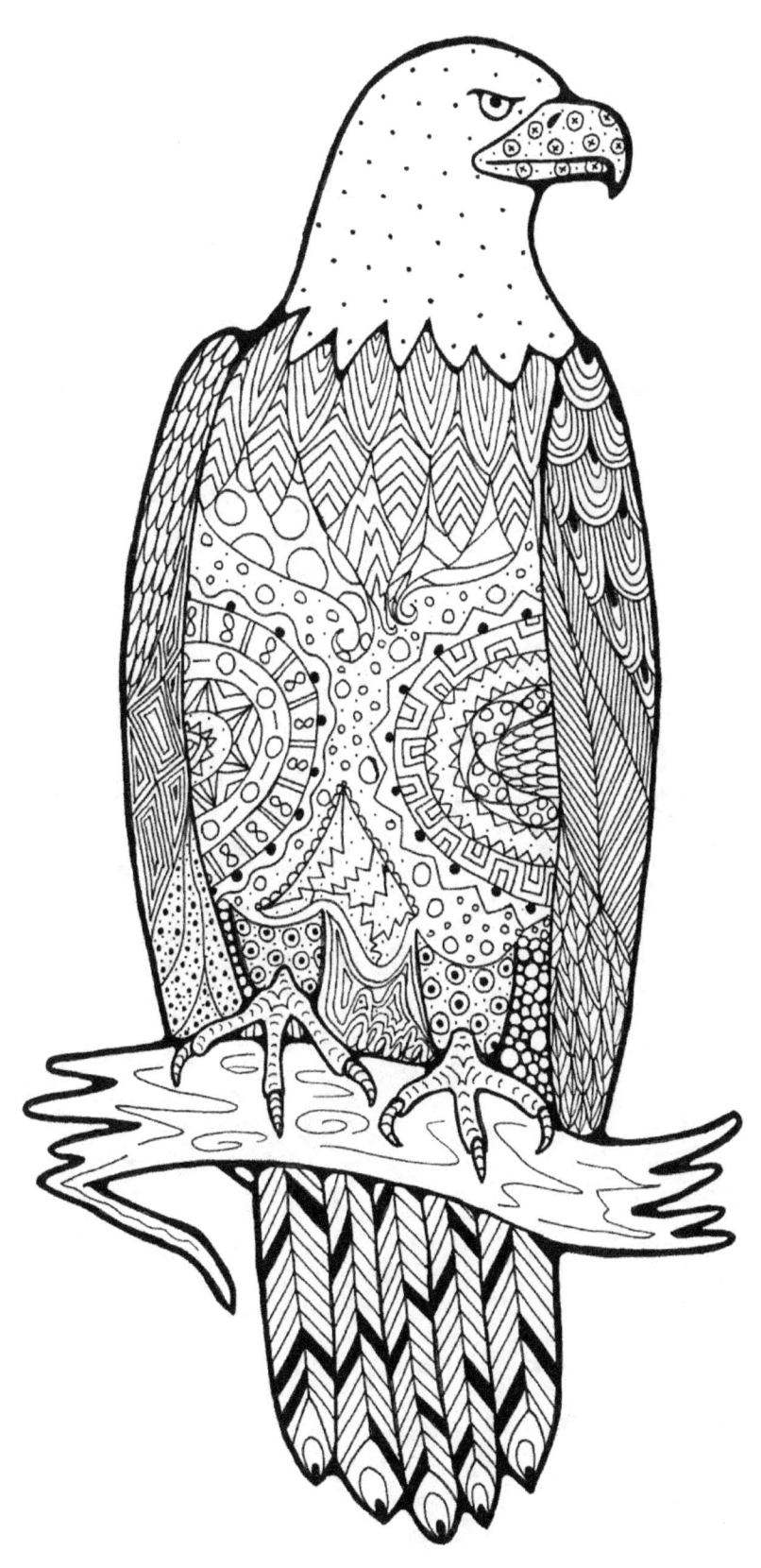

Bald Eagle

Fun Fact: The white of the head and tail
develops over the course of 5 years.

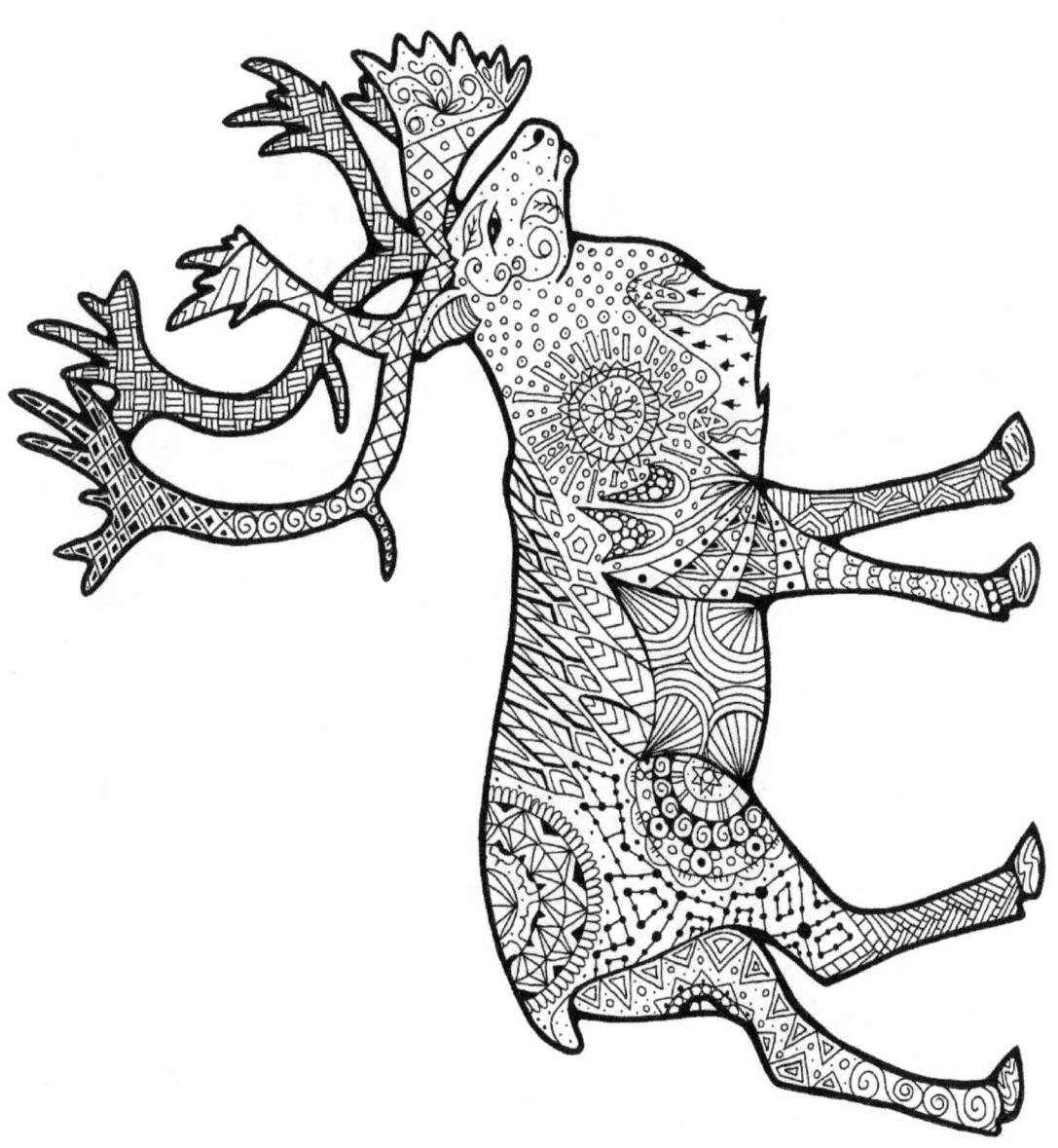

Caribou

Fun Fact: Domesticated caribou are known as reindeer.

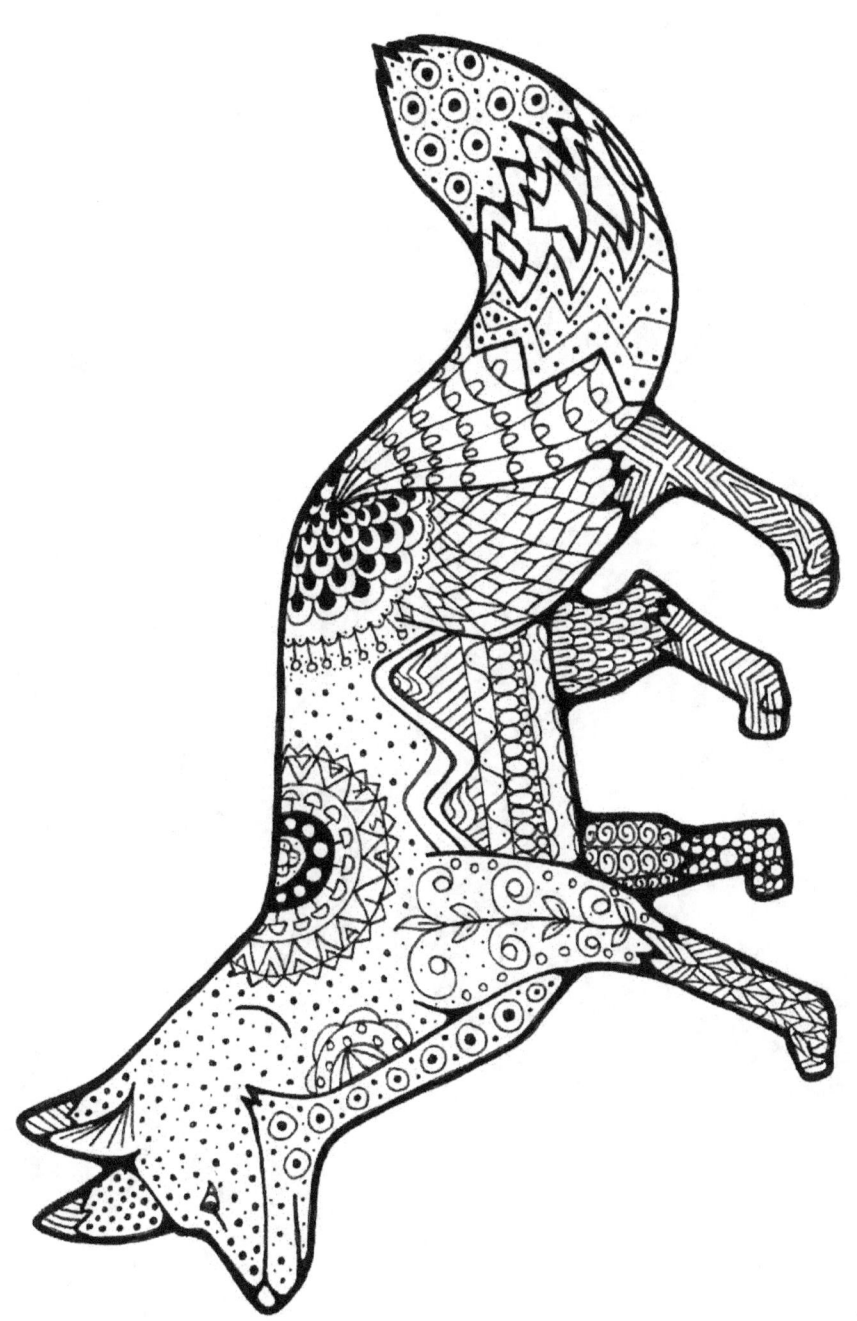

Red Fox

Fun Fact: The female fox is called a 'vixen', and a baby
fox is called a 'kit'.

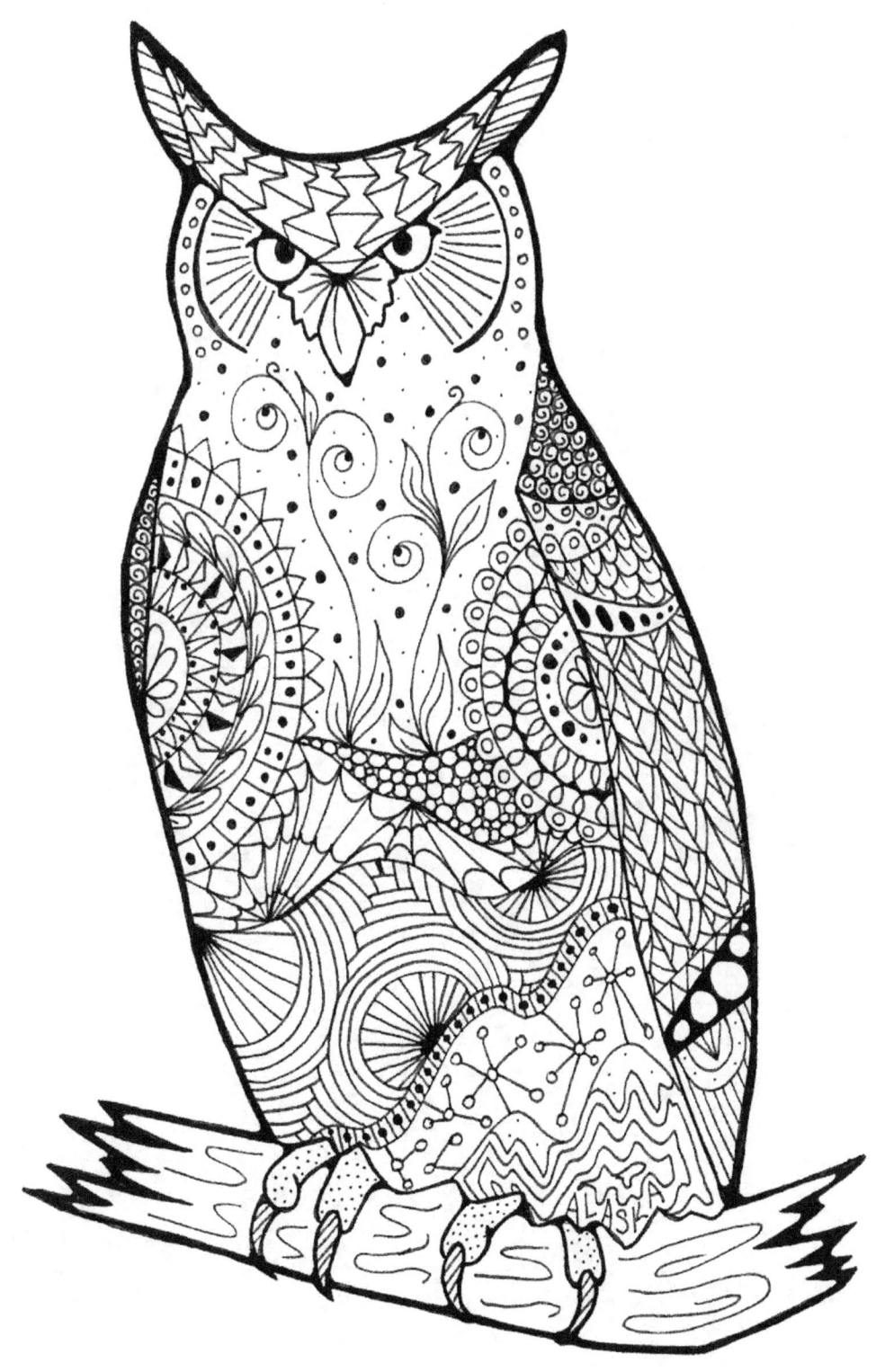

Horned Owl

Fun Fact: Females are usually larger than their male
counterparts.

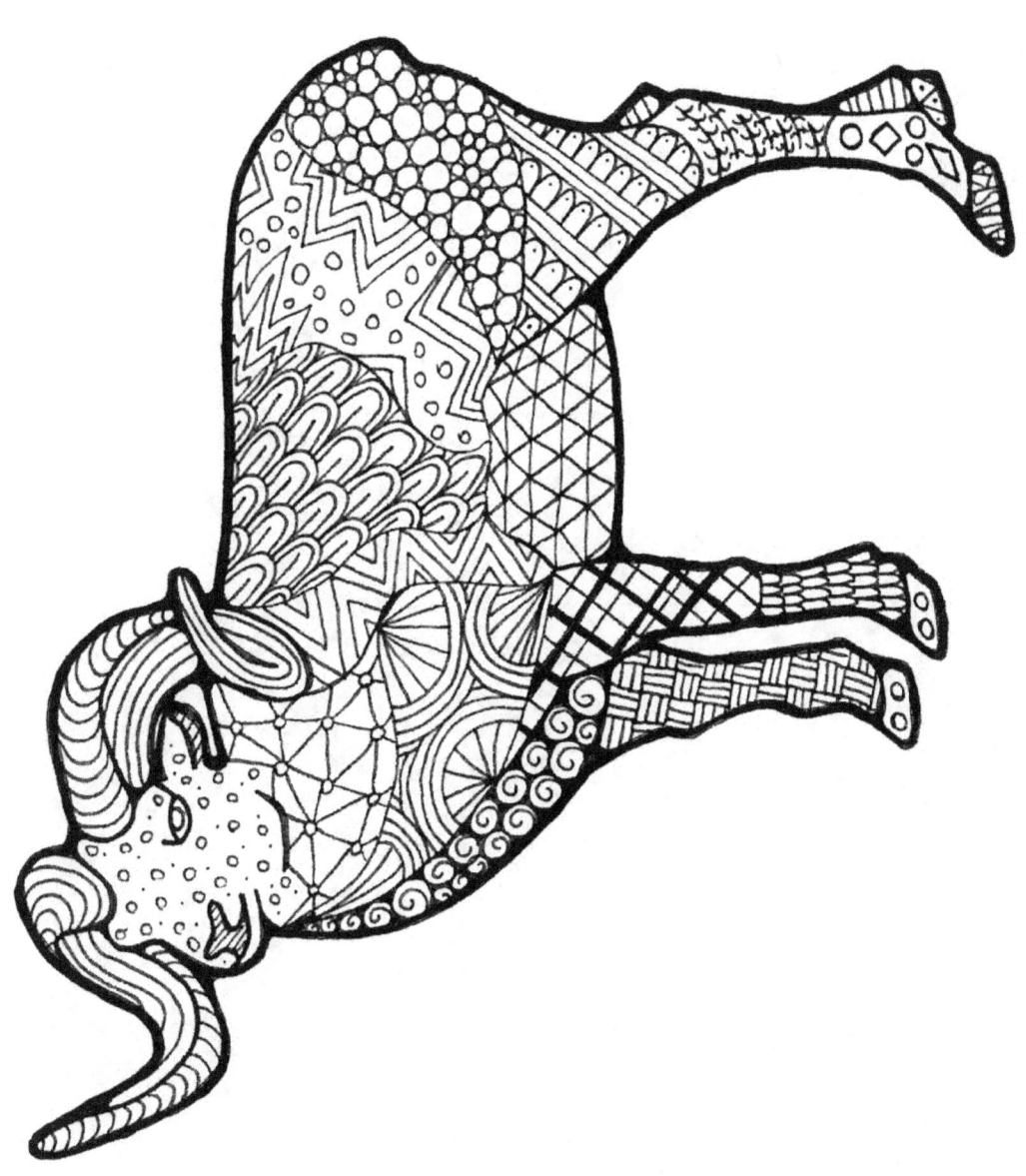

Dall Sheep

Fun Fact: Dall sheep are herbivores that can weigh
up to 300 pounds.

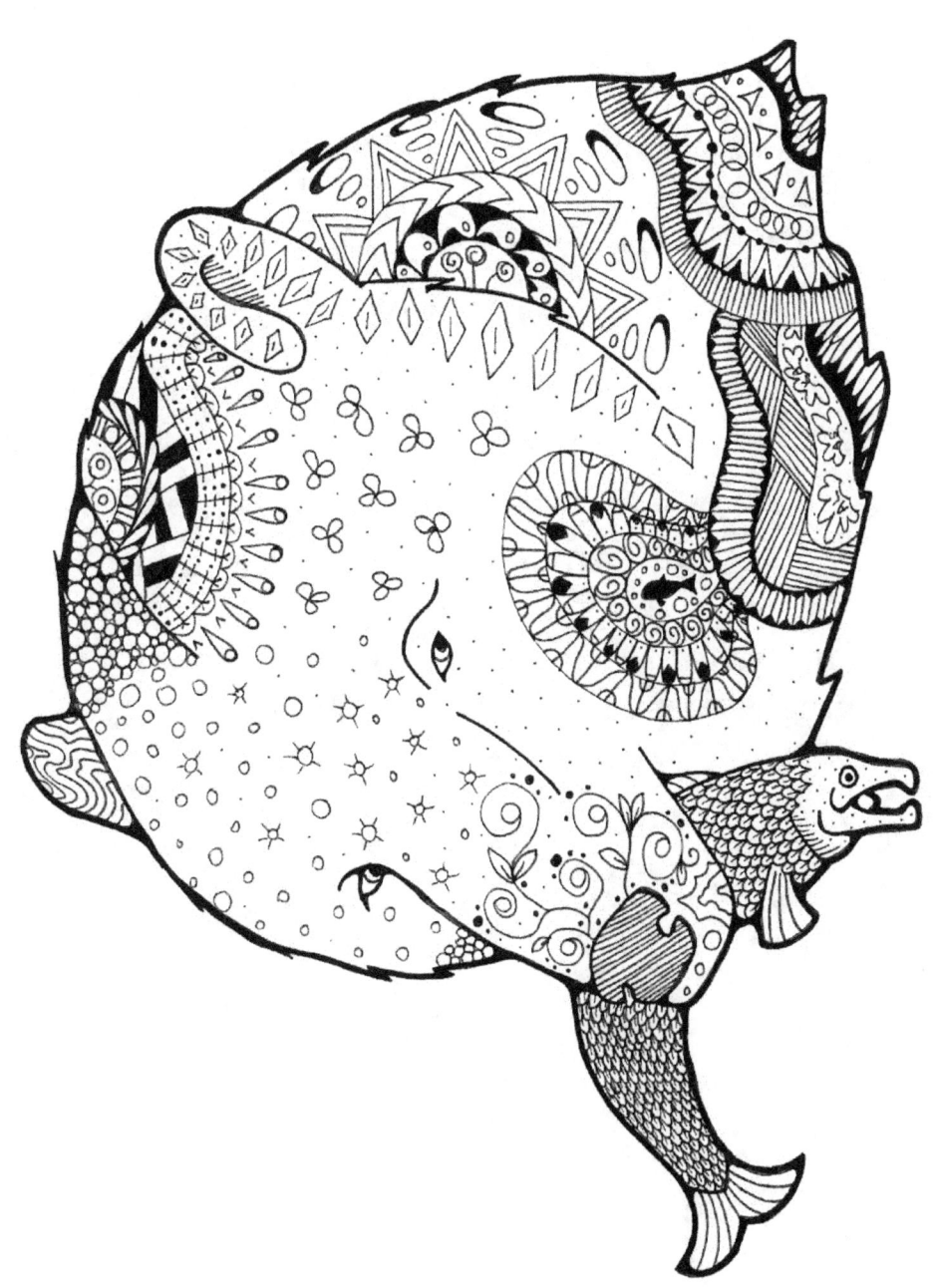

Brown Bear with Salmon

Fun Fact: Brown bears tend to live along the
southern coast of Alaska, near salmon-spawning
areas.

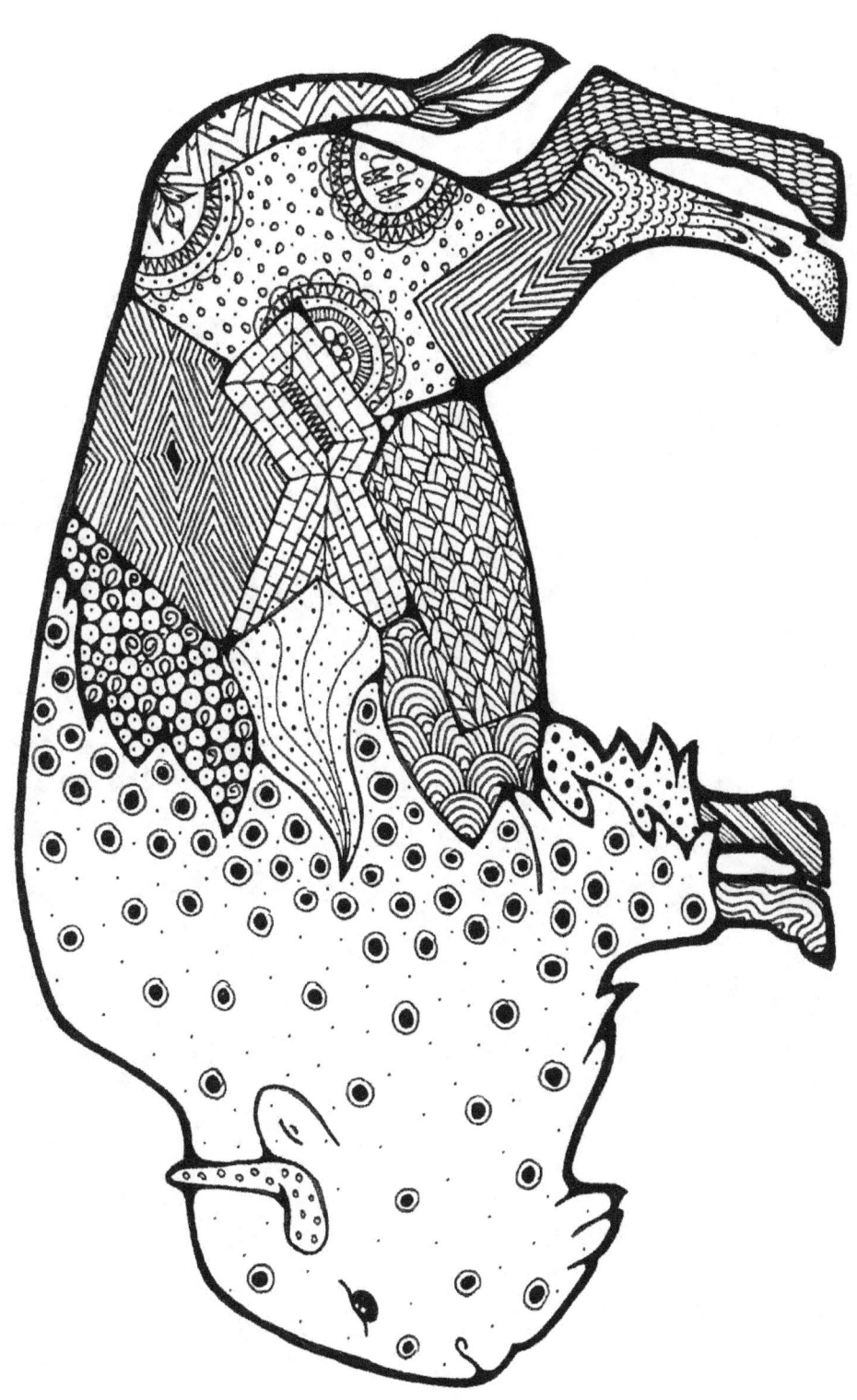

Bison

Fun Fact: Bison almost became extinct in Alaska
in the 1800's, but the population is healthy now.

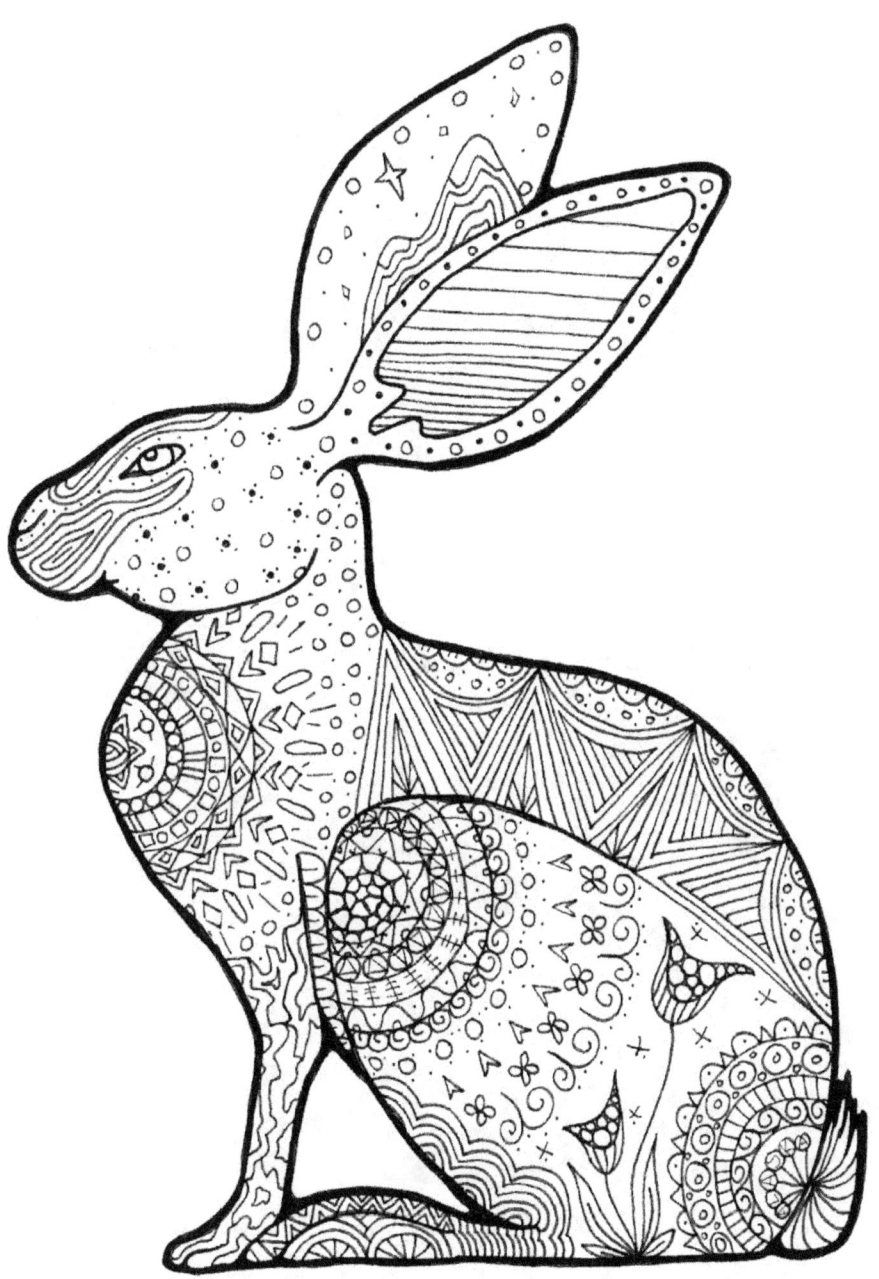

Snowshoe Hare

Fun Fact: The hind feet of a snowshoe hare have a lot of fur, this helps them move through deep snow easier.

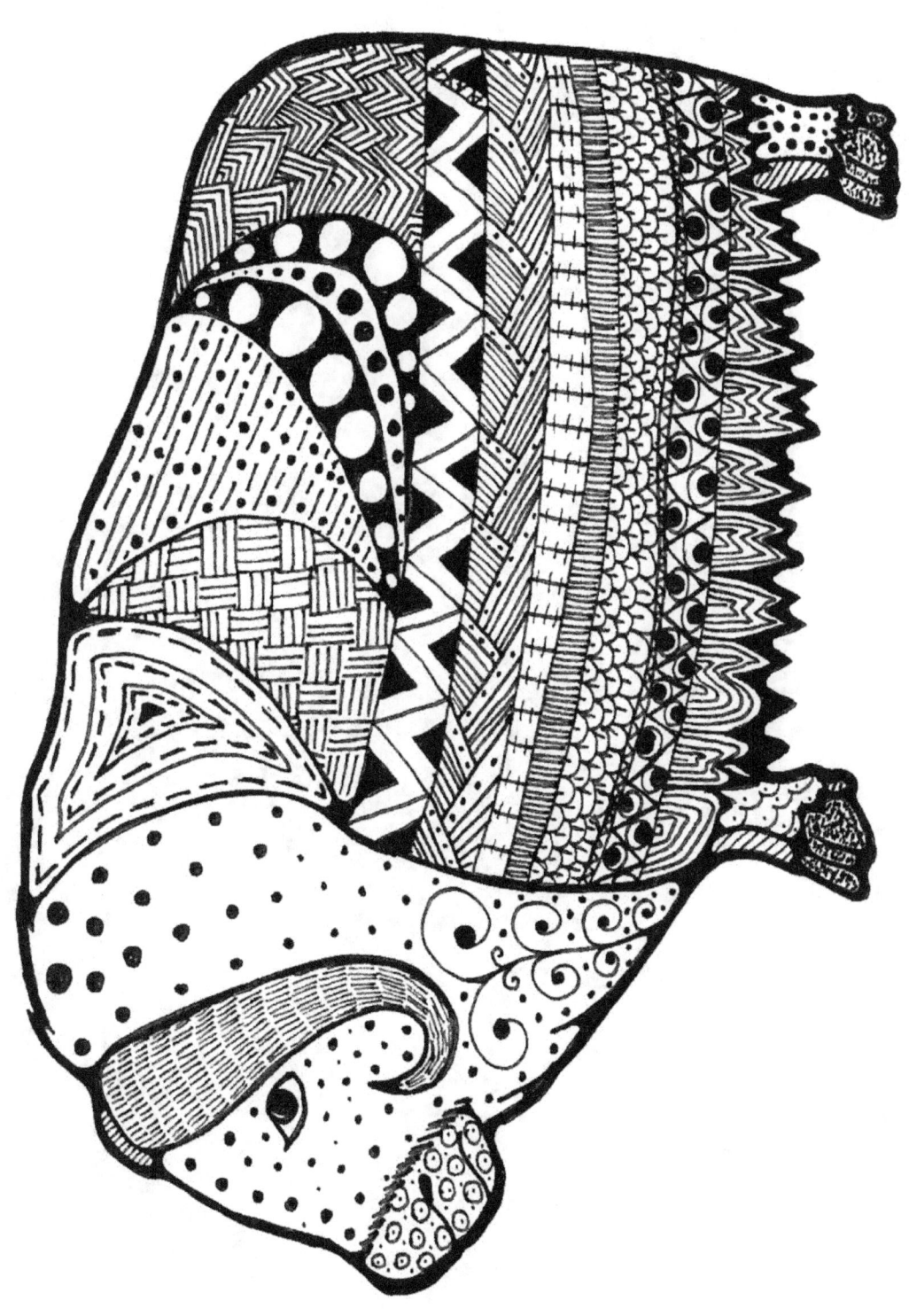

Musk Ox

Fun Fact: The underfur of a musk ox is called qiviut and is
very expensive.

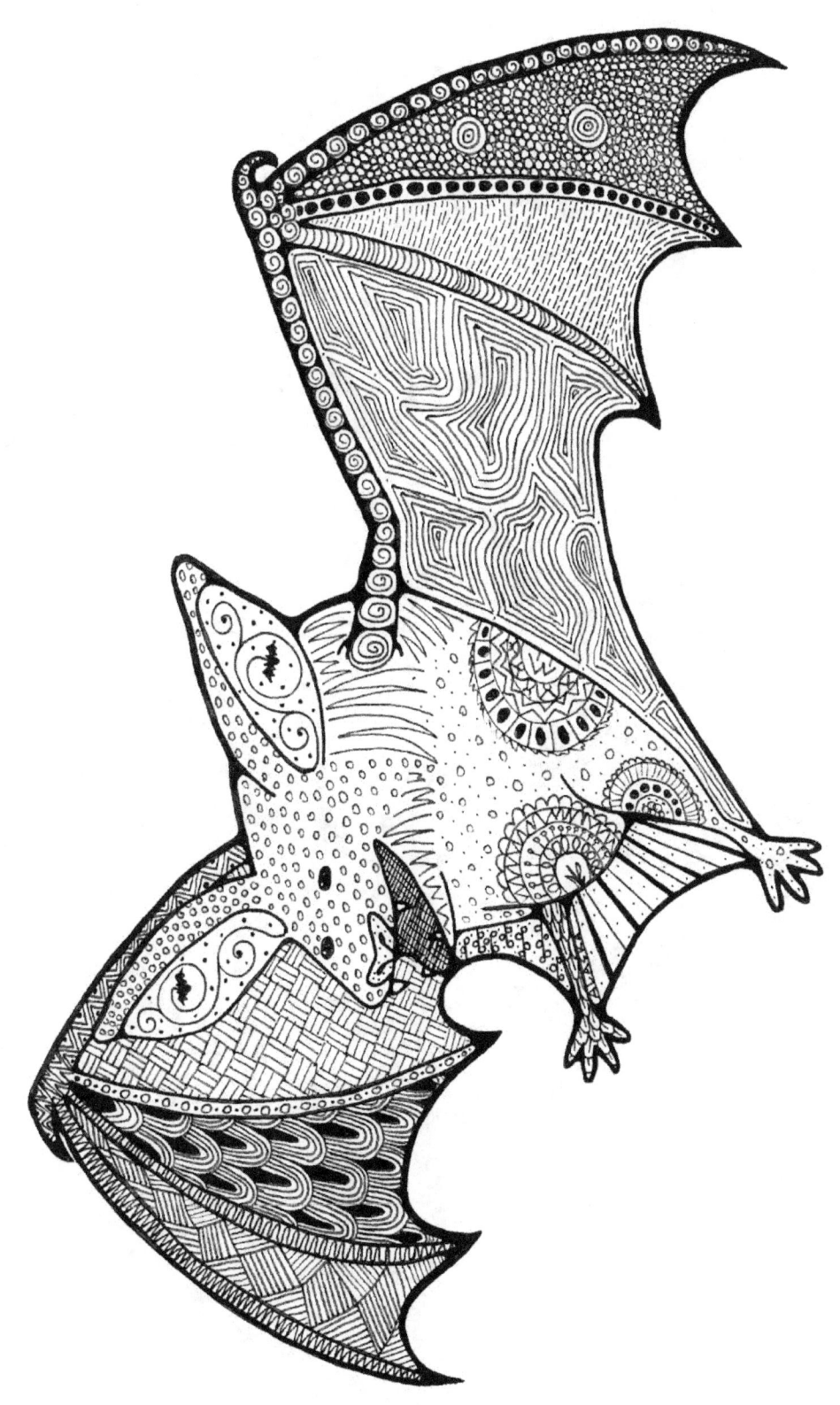

Bat

Fun Fact: Bats are found throughout Alaska, with the exception of the north and most of the islands.

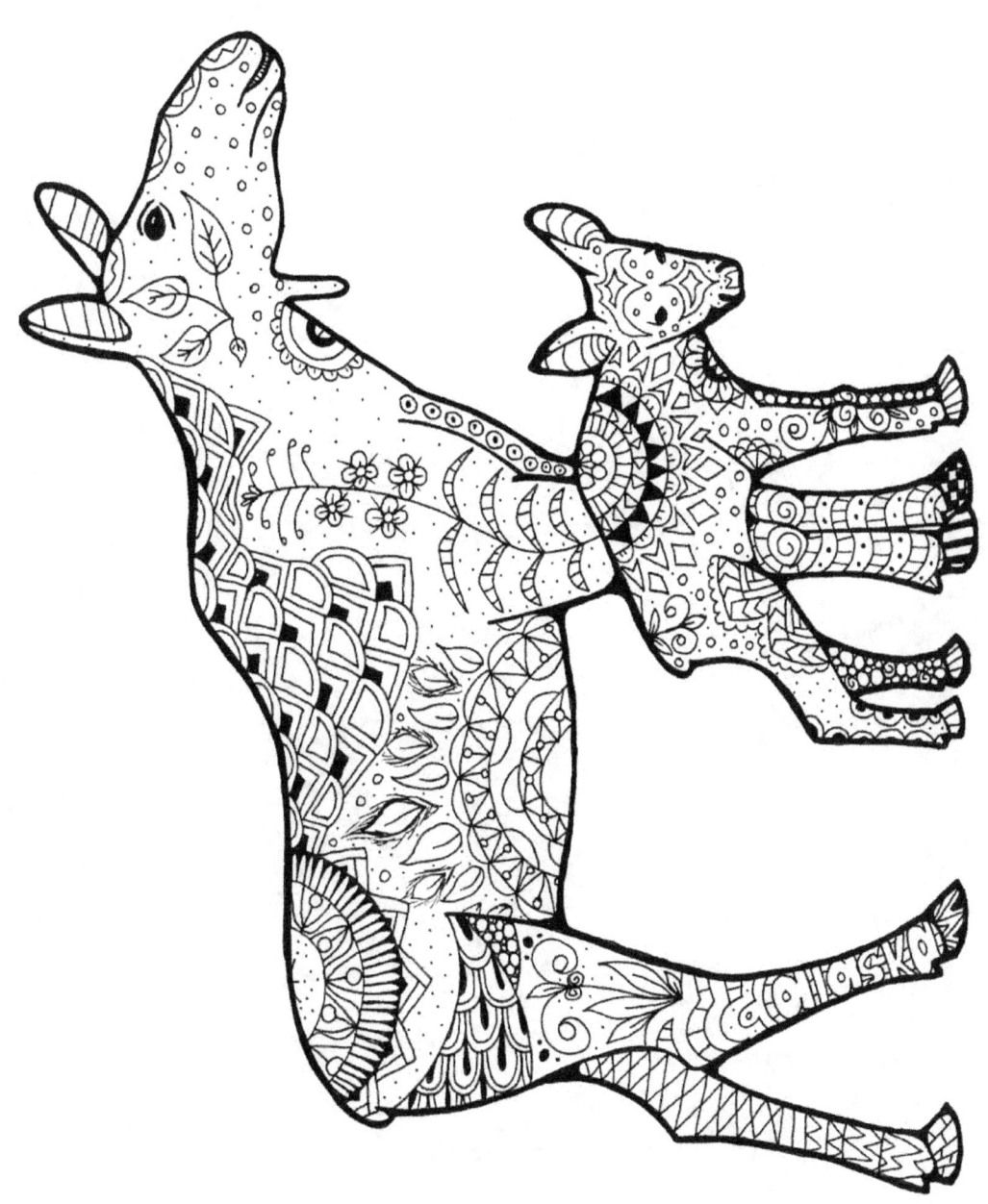

Moose Cow and Calf

Fun Fact: Young moose mature to adulthood at 4-6 years.

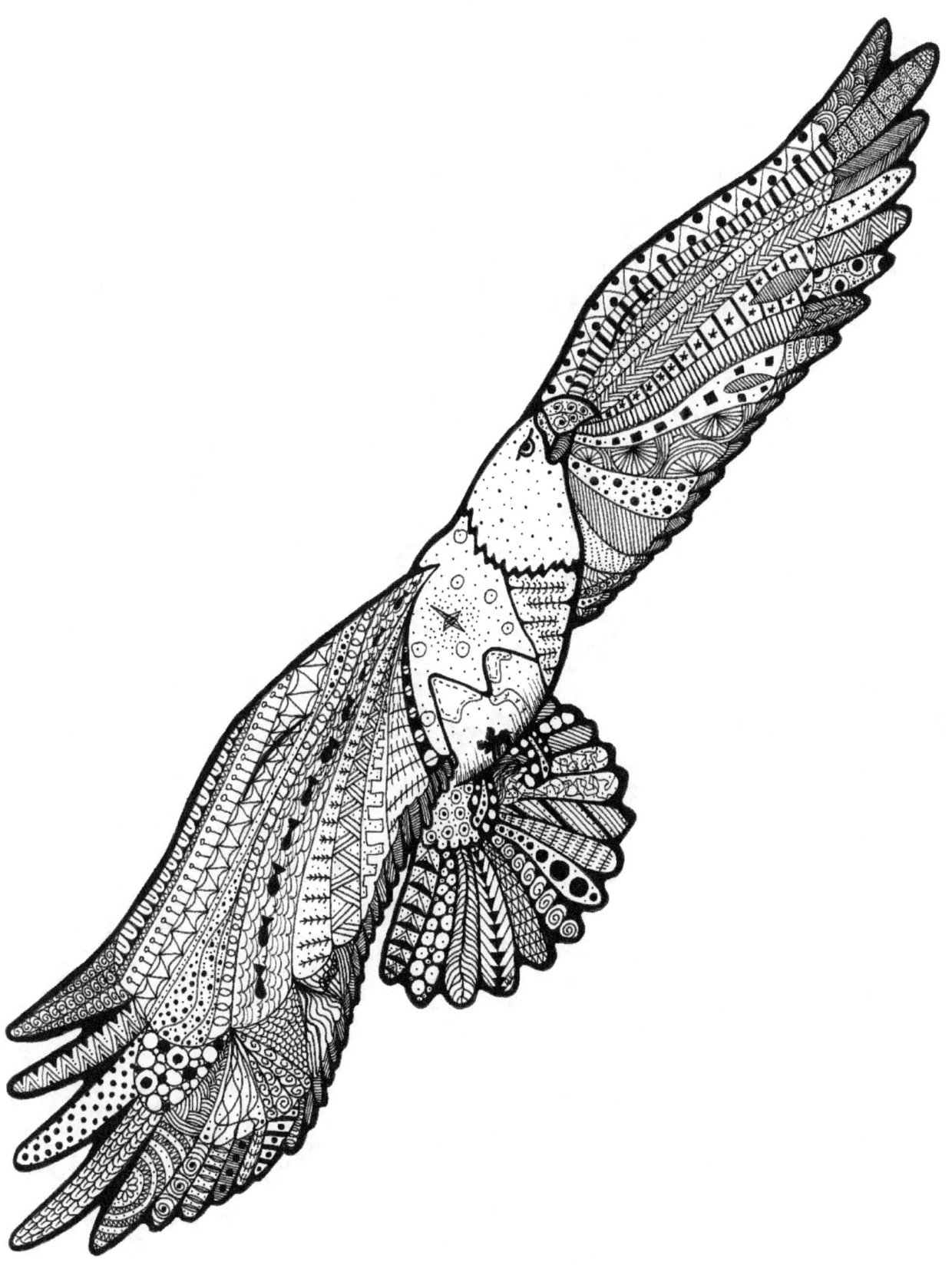

Soaring Bald Eagle

Fun Fact: There are about 30,000 bald eagles in Alaska.

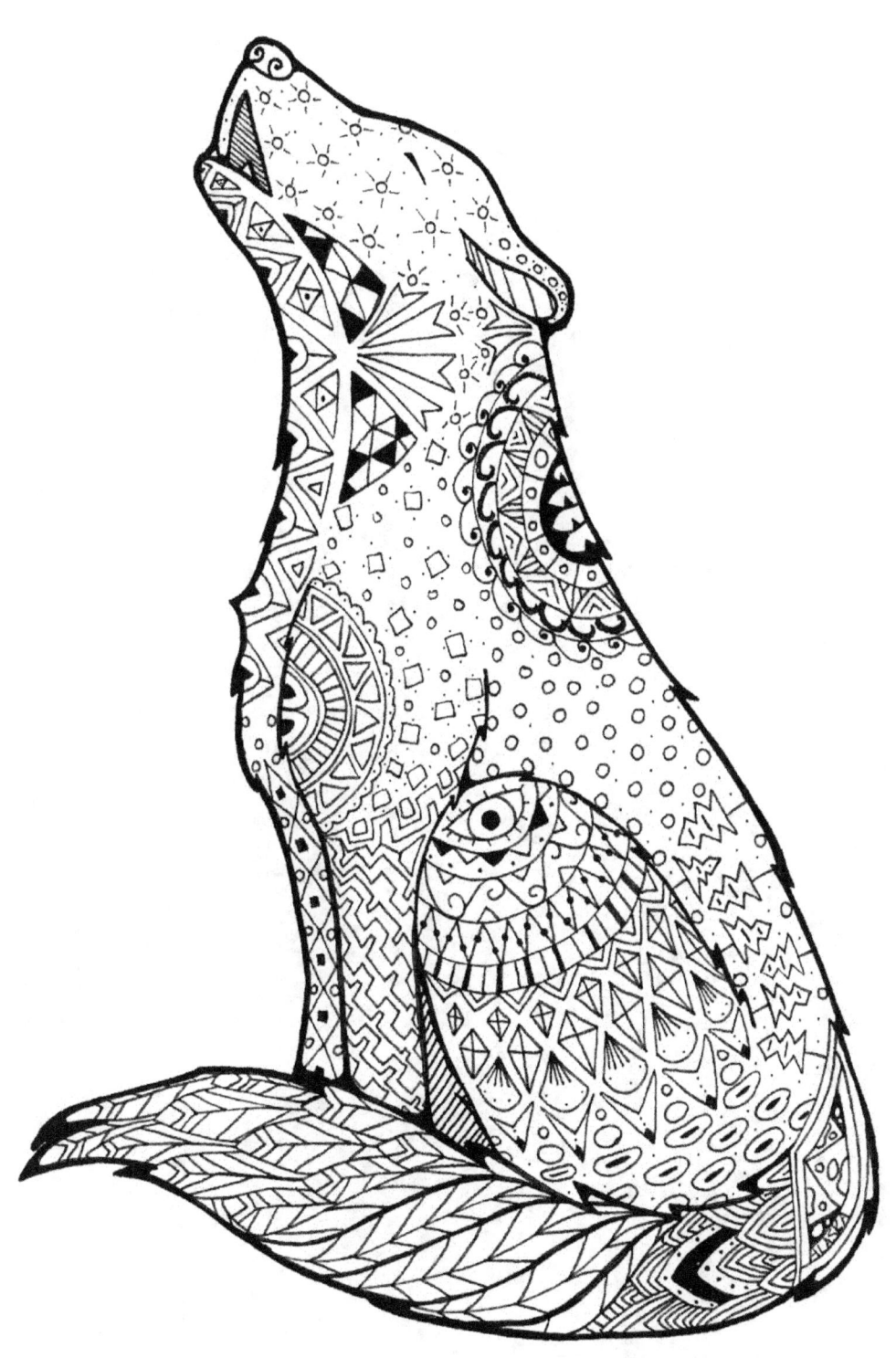

Wolf

Fun Fact: Wolves are carnivores that prefer big game animals such as moose and caribou.

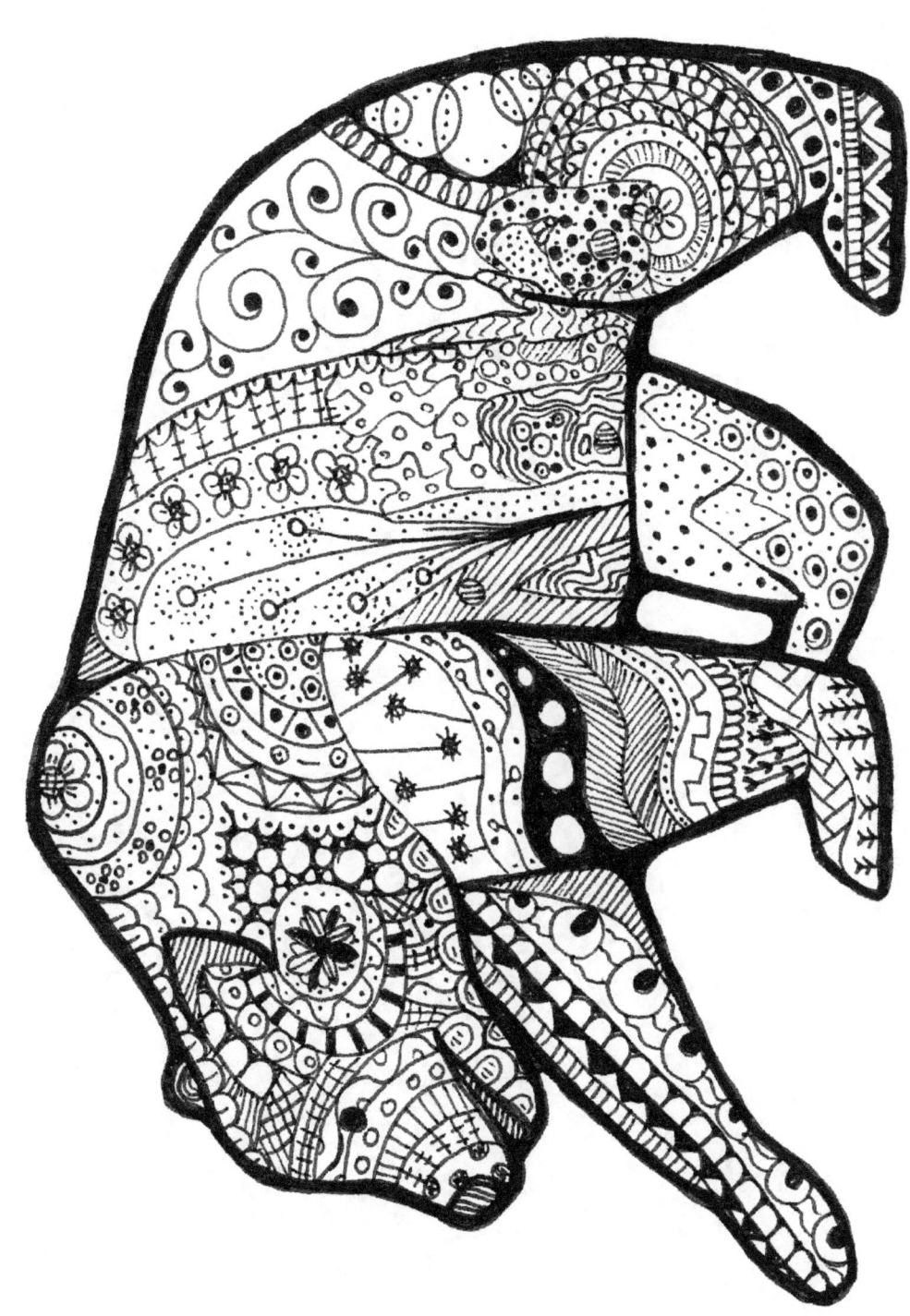

Black Bear

Fun Fact: Black bears are smaller and have shorter claws than brown bears.

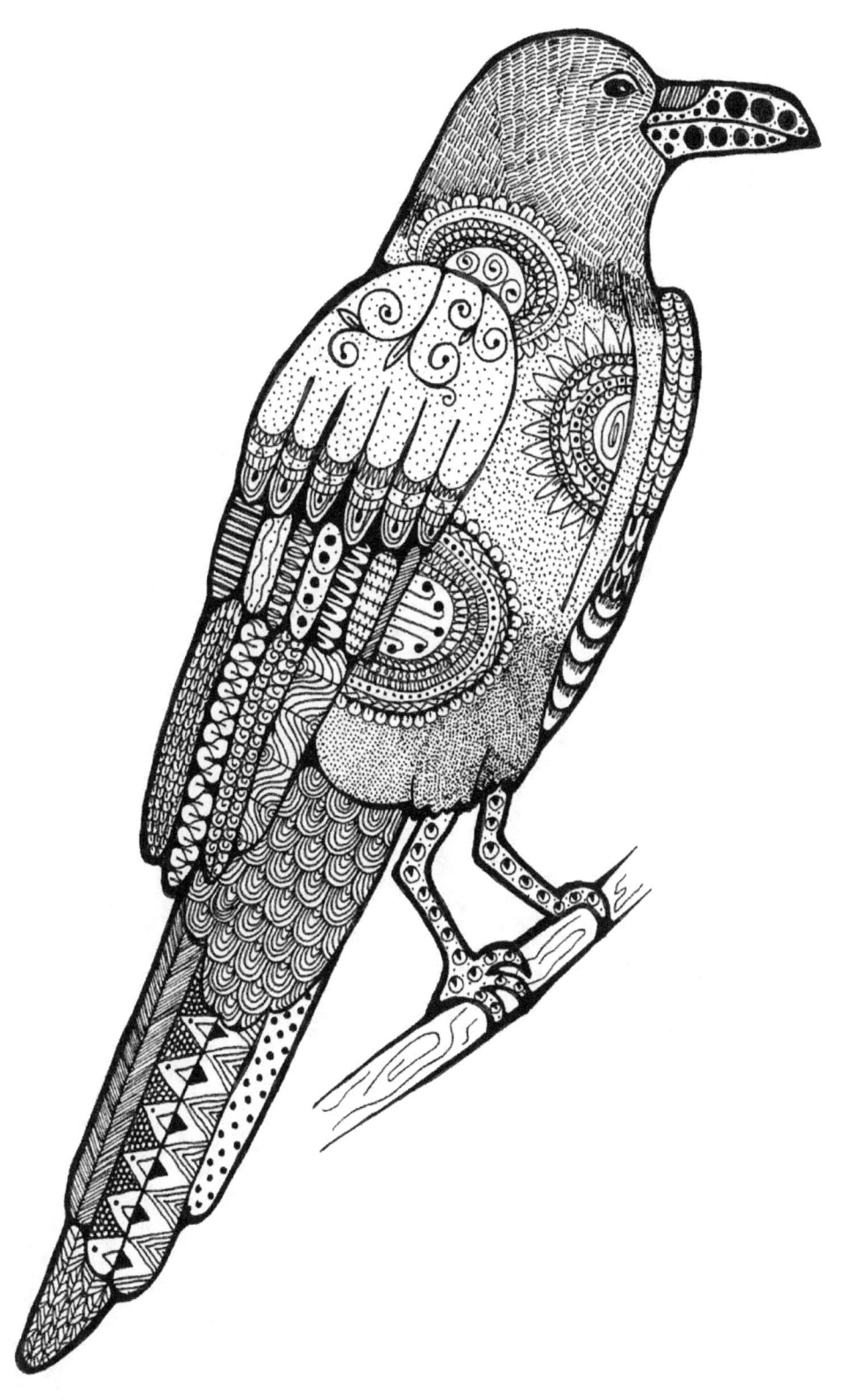

Common Raven

Fun Fact: Raven populations flourish near more
developed areas, where human activity is more common.

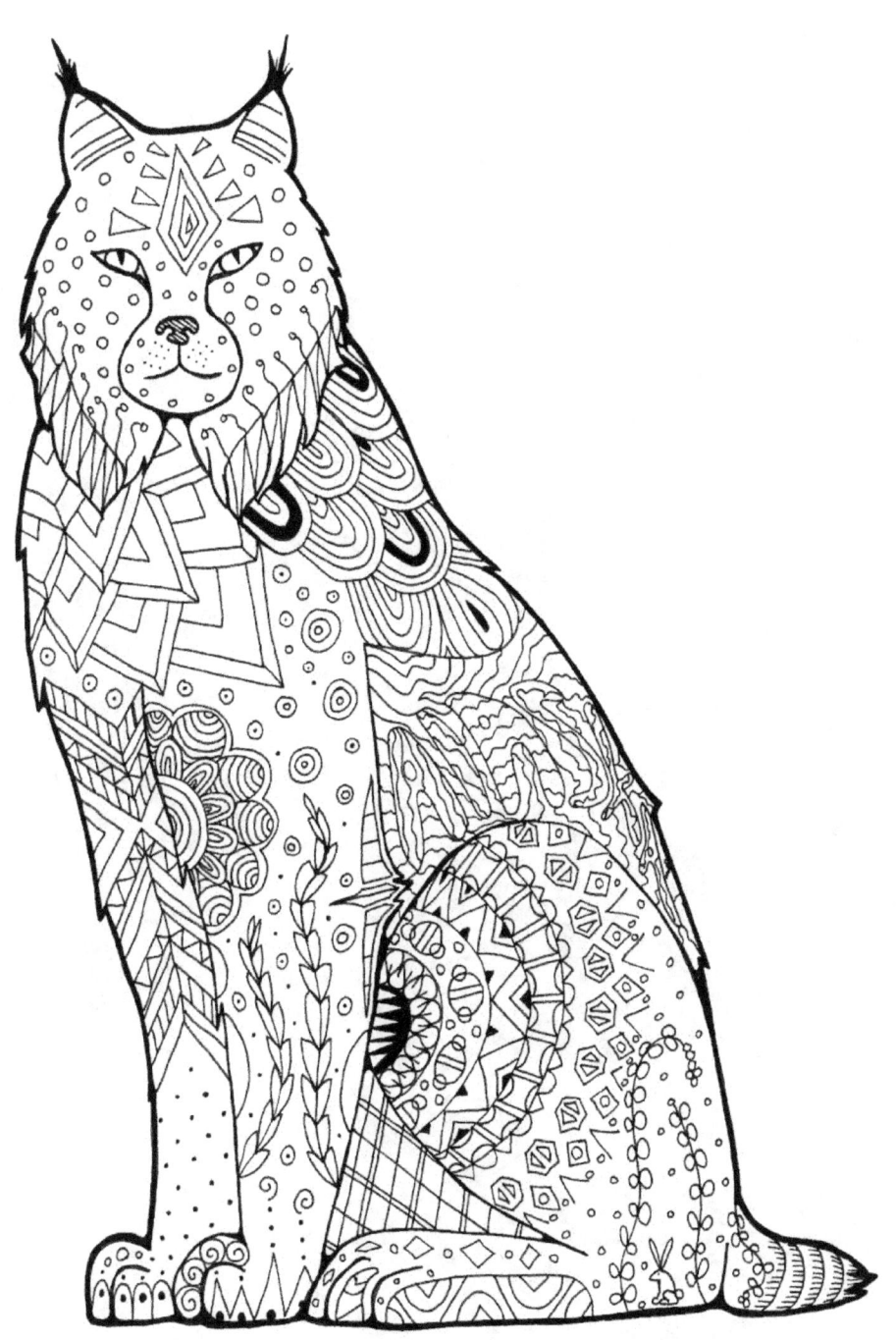

Lynx

Fun Fact: Lynx prefer to eat hare, and are found to be more common near hare-populated areas.

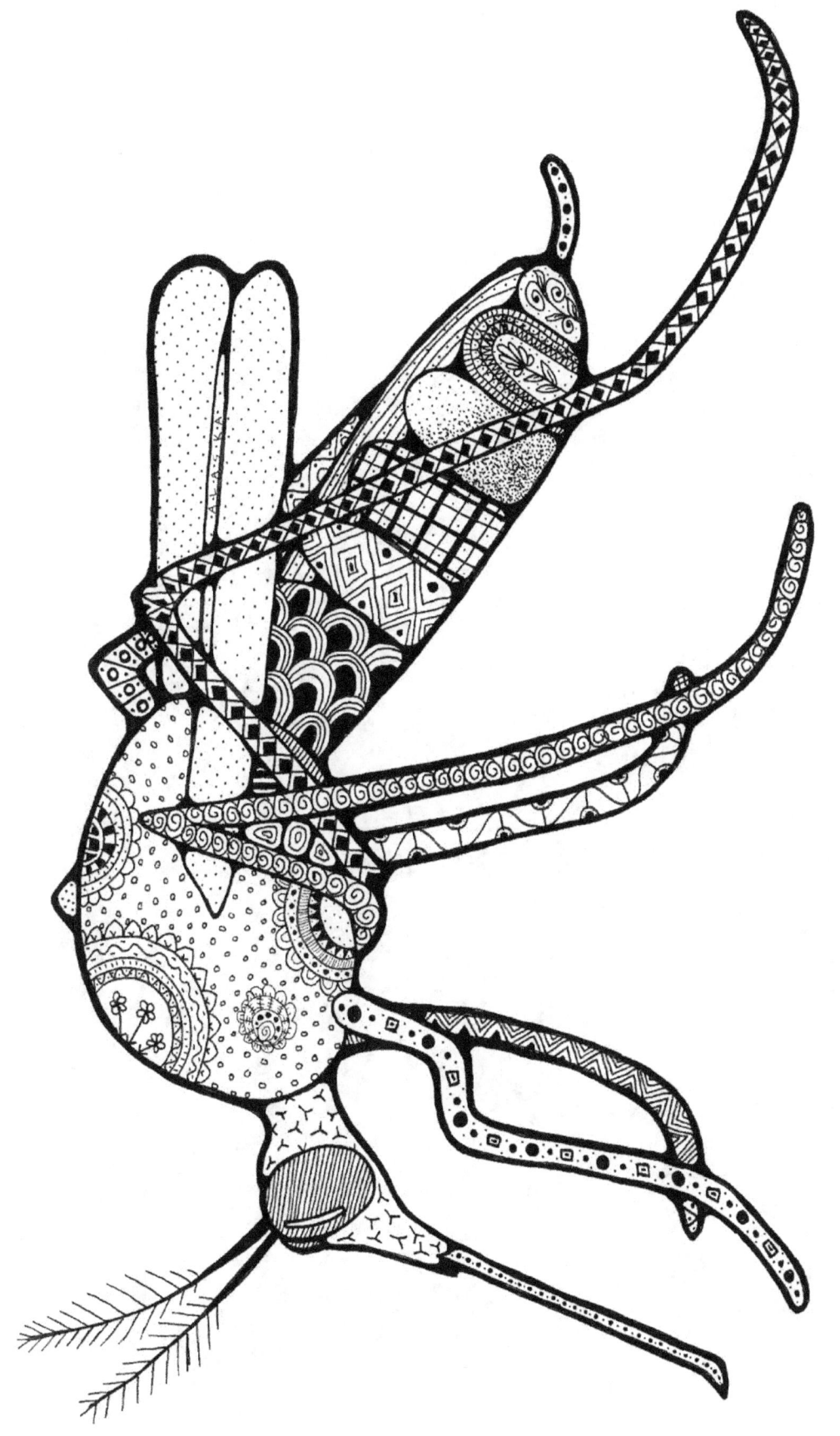

Mosquito

Fun Fact: Only female mosquitoes bite. Mosquitoes
are jokingly referred to as the Alaska state bird.

About the Artist

Brittney is a former Army brat, turned Alaskan artist from Palmer (home to giant cabbage and the Alaska State Fair). She lives with her much-loved pets and she loves living the Alaskan life. Brittney has always been the creative one in her family, crafting things since she was a child (She even has her 6th grade portfolio, full of wonderful works). She began drawing her animals and other special projects about 2 years ago and found it very soothing. She hopes you find this coloring book as fun and relaxing as she does. To keep up with her future and present projects, like her page on Facebook: www.facebook.com/artbybrittneyk

If you are interested in a custom drawing or prices on art prints, please visit inkedfoxbybrittney.com or you may e-mail inkedfoxak@gmail.com

Finding Alaska: A Little Help

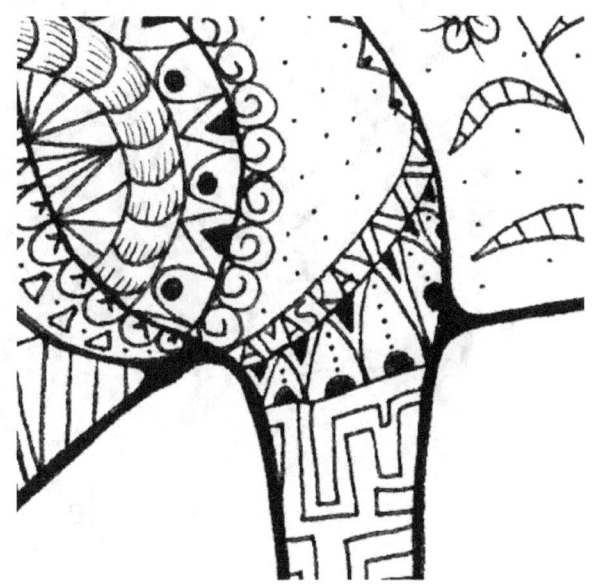

Bull Moose

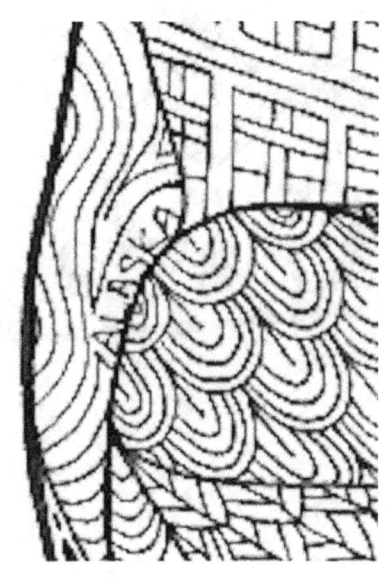

Willow Ptarmigan

Mountain Goat

Brown Bear

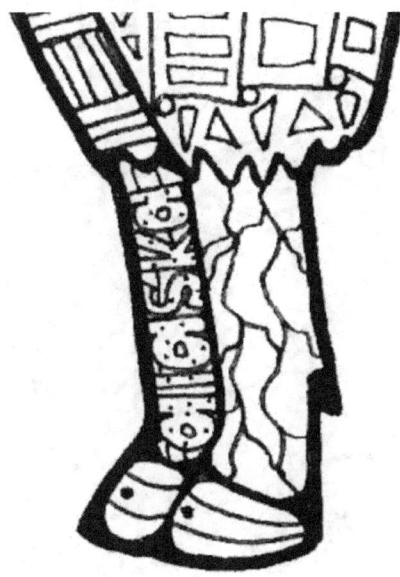

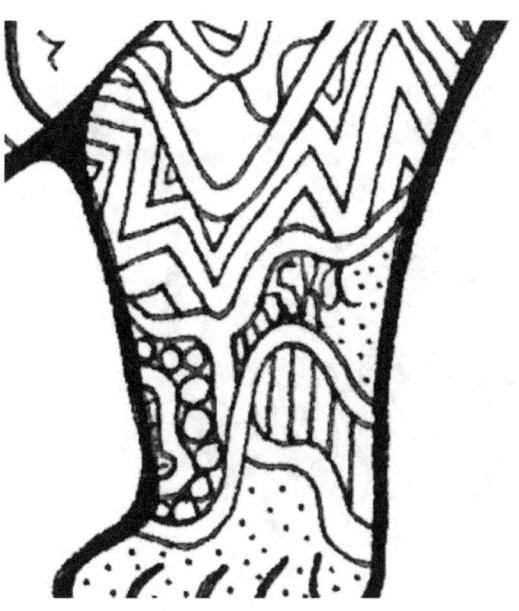

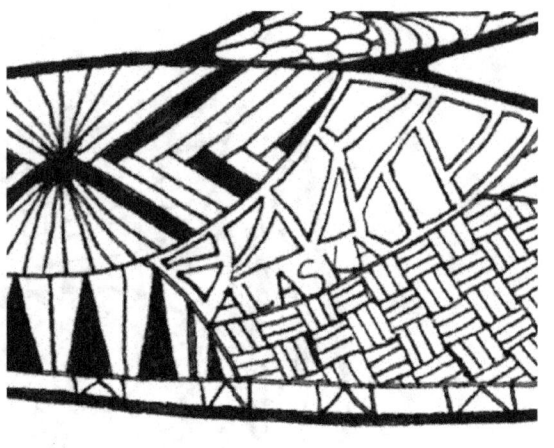

Dragonfly

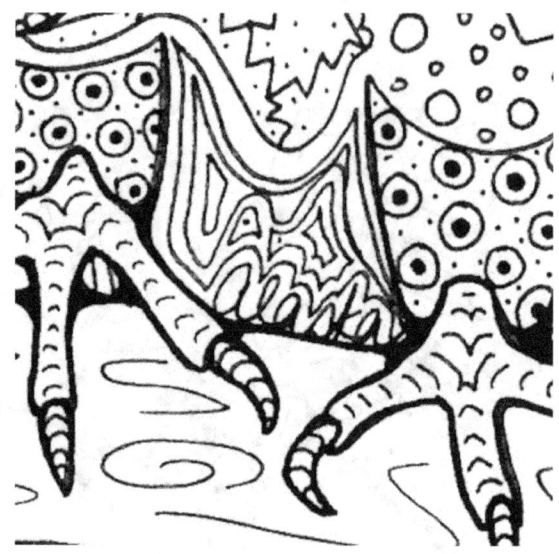

Perched Bald Eagle

Caribou

Red Fox

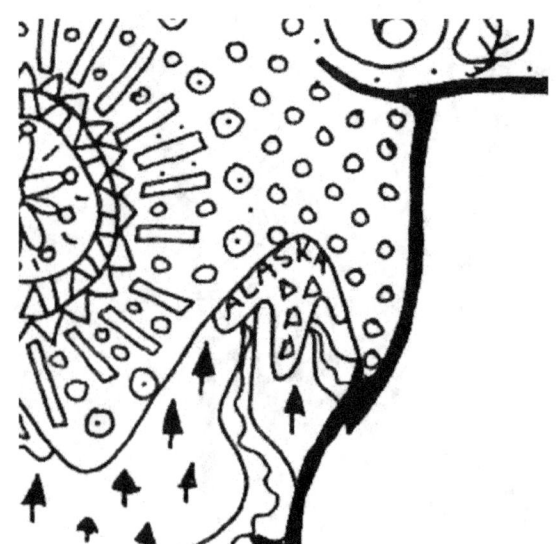

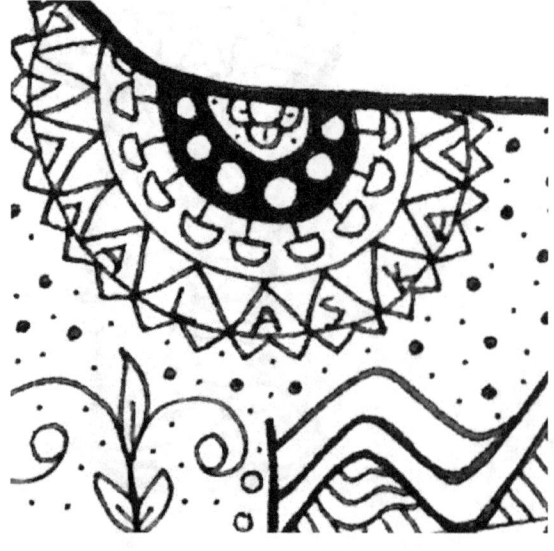

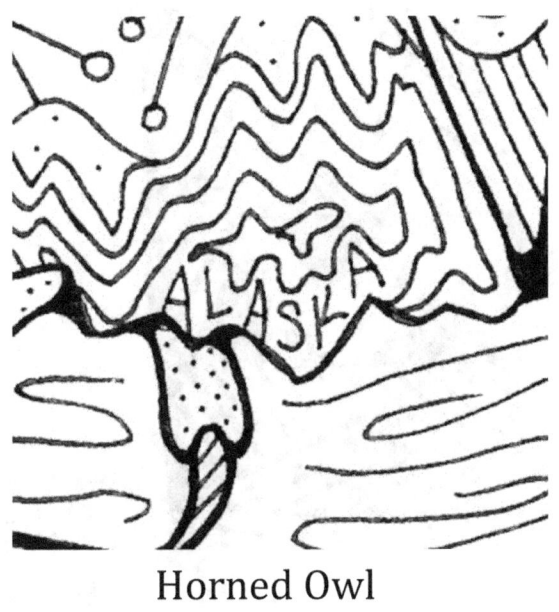

Horned Owl

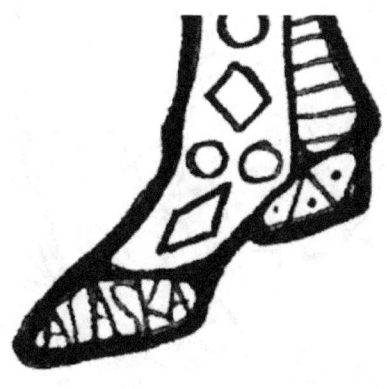

Dall Sheep

Brown Bear with Salmon

Bison

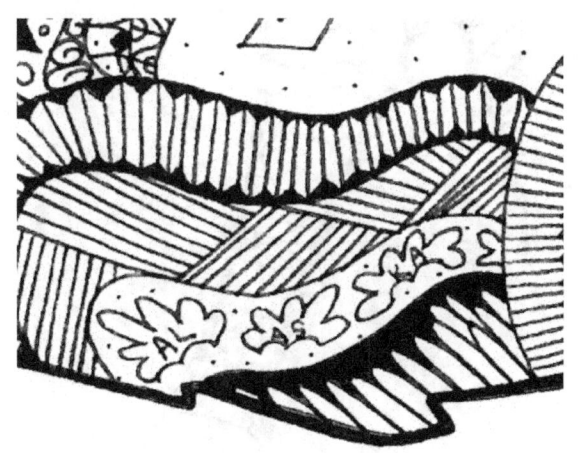

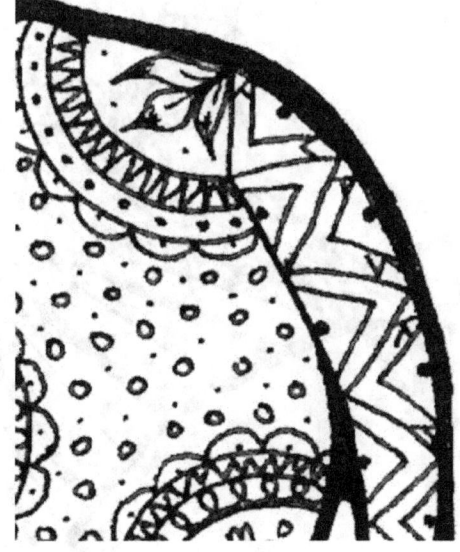

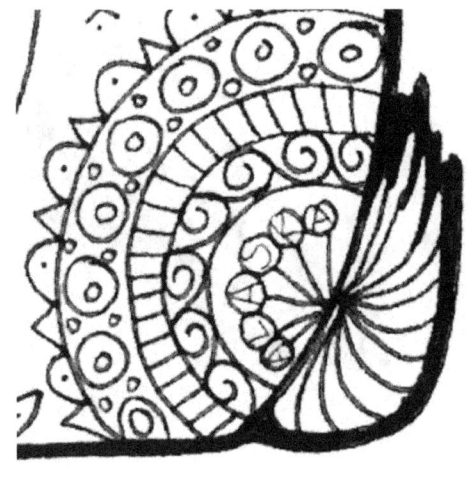

Snowshoe Hare

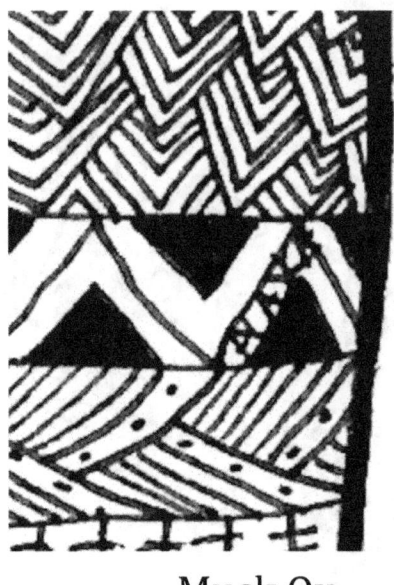

Musk Ox

Bat

Moose Cow and Calf

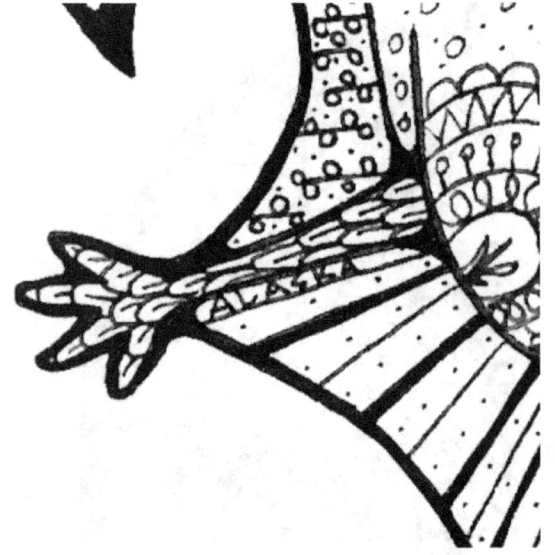

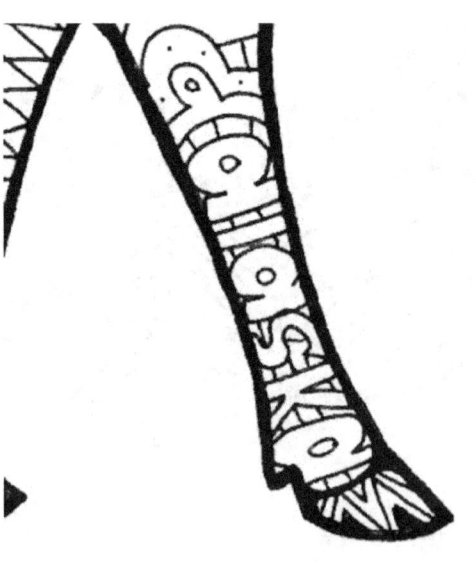

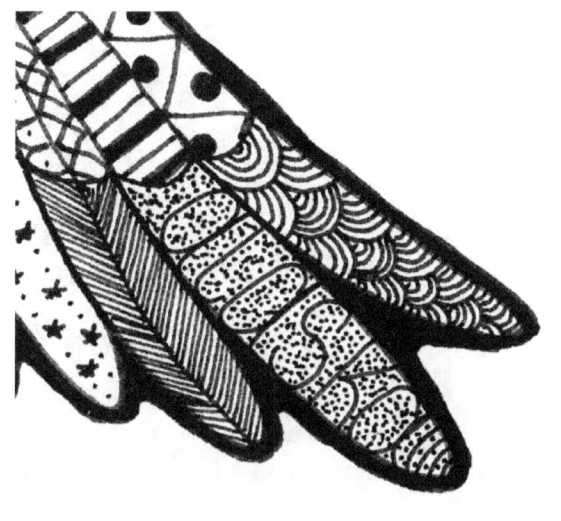

Soaring Bald Eagle

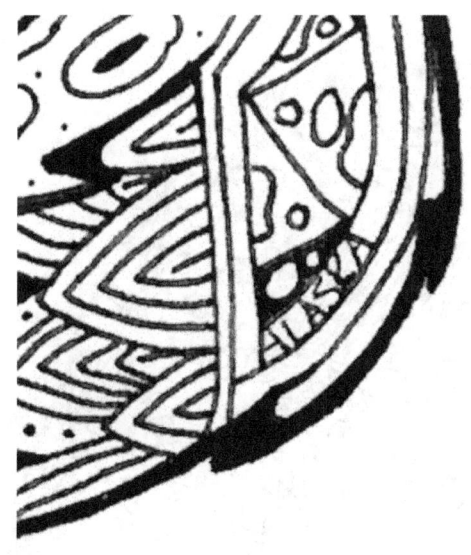

Wolf

Black Bear

Common Raven

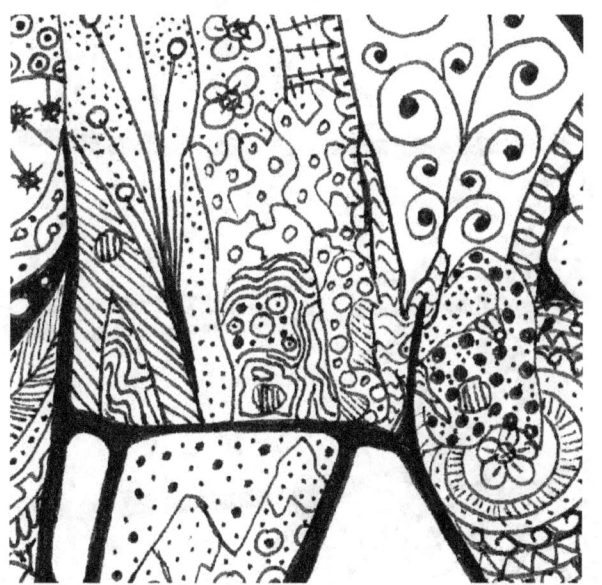

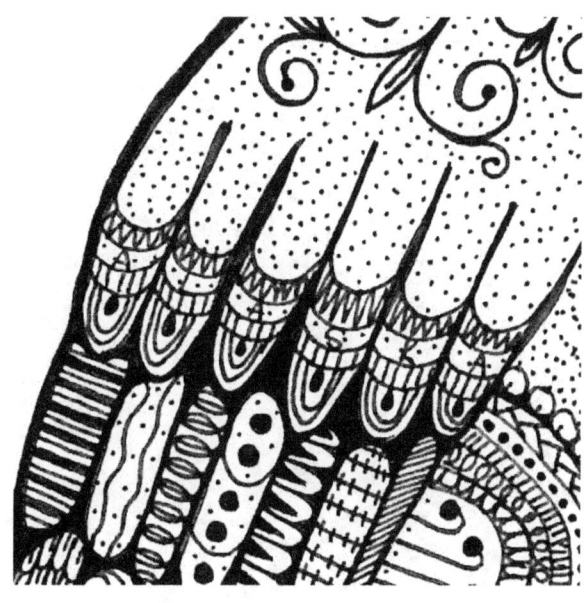

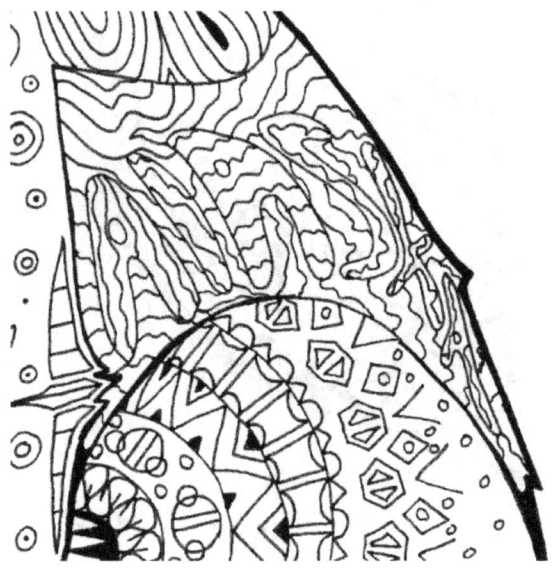

Lynx

Mosquito

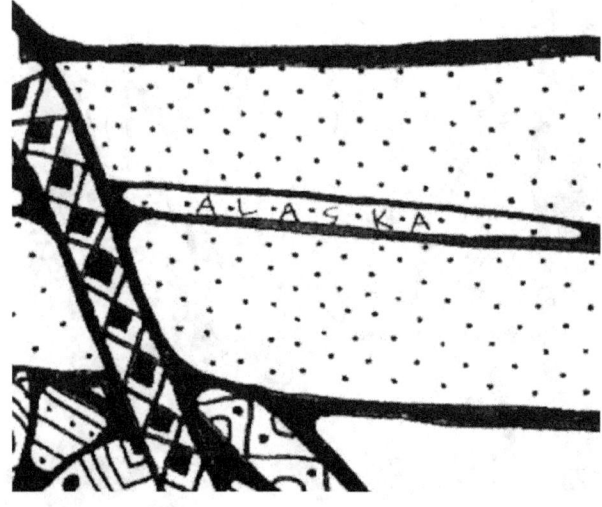